Gluten-Free Air Fryer Recipe Book

Elevate Your Zero Gluten Cooking with Delicious and Nutritious Meal Prep Using Air Fryer Techniques

PEARL M. HARRISON

Copyright © [2023] [Pearl M. Harrison]

All rights reserved. No portion of this book may be copied without the publisher's consent, saved in a database, or transmitted in any way, whether it be electronically, mechanically, photocopying, recording, or otherwise.

[Pearl M. Harrison]

Table Of Contents

Introduction

Chapter One: Gluten-Free

About The Gluten Free

Gluten-Free Air Fryer Cooking

Science of Gluten-Free

Chapter Two: Basics of Gluten-Free Air Fryer Cooking

Vegetables

Chicken

Fish

Chapter Three: Choosing The Best Air Fryer

Chapter Four: Breakfast Recipes

Gluten-Free Air Fryer Omelet:

Gluten-Free Air Fryer Pancakes:

Gluten-Free Air Fryer Breakfast Sandwich:

Gluten-Free Sweet Potato Hash Browns:

Gluten-Free Air Fryer Breakfast Potatoes:

Gluten-Free Air Fryer Granola Bars:

Gluten-Free Air Fryer Breakfast Sausage Patties:

Gluten-Free Air Fryer Egg Muffins:

Gluten-Free Air Fryer Breakfast Quiche:

Gluten-Free Air Fryer Bacon:
Gluten-Free Air Fryer French Toast:

Chapter Five: Snacks and Appetizers
Gluten-Free Air Fryer Mozzarella Sticks:
Gluten-Free Air Fryer Buffalo Wings:
Gluten-Free Air Fryer Jalapeno Poppers:
Gluten-Free Air Fryer Pickles:
Gluten-Free Air Fryer Plantain Chips:
Gluten-Free Air Fryer Falafel:
Gluten-Free Air Fryer Broccoli Bites:
Gluten-Free Air Fryer Onion Rings:
Gluten-Free Air Fryer Avocado Fries:

Chapter Six: Main Courses
Gluten-Free Air Fryer Fried Chicken:
Gluten-Free Air Fryer Steak Fajitas:
Gluten-Free Air Fryer Shrimp Scampi:
Gluten-Free Air Fryer Brussels Sprouts:
Gluten-Free Air Fryer Tofu Skewers:
Gluten-Free Air Fryer Salmon Filets:

Chapter Seven: Sides and Vegetable Dishes
Gluten-Free Air Fryer Roasted Vegetables:

Gluten-Free Sweet Potato Fries:
Gluten-Free Air Fryer Zucchini Chips:
Gluten-Free Air Fryer Fried Green Potatoes:
Gluten-Free Air Fryer Grilled Corn on the Cob:
Gluten-Free Air Fryer Asparagus:
Gluten-Free Air Fryer Artichokes:
Gluten-Free Air Fryer Peppers:
Gluten-Free Air Fryer Mushrooms:
Gluten-Free Air Fryer Green Beans:
Gluten-Free Air Fryer Eggplant:

Chapter Eight: Desserts
Gluten-Free Air Fryer Apple Chips:
Gluten-Free Air Fryer Chocolate Chip Cookies:
Gluten-Free Air Fryer Brownies:
Gluten-Free Air Fryer Banana Bread:
Gluten-Free Air Fryer Peach Crisp:
Gluten-Free Air Fryer Peanut Butter Cookies:
Gluten-Free Air Fryer Donuts:
Gluten-Free Air Fryer Lemon Bars:

Chapter Nine: Sauces Dressings and Staples
Gluten-Free Air Fryer Barbeque Sauce:
Gluten-Free Ranch Air Fryer Dressing:

Gluten-Free Air Fryer Lemon Vinaigrette:
Gluten-Free Air Fryer Teriyaki Sauce:
Gluten-free air fryer pesto:
Gluten-free air fryer buffalo sauce:

Chapter Ten: Meat and Seafood
Gluten-Free Air Fryer Chicken Tenders:
Gluten-Free Air Fryer Shrimp:
Gluten-Free Air Fryer Pork Chops:
Gluten-Free Air Fryer Salmon:
Gluten-Free Air Fryer Turkey:
Gluten-Free Air Fryer Crab Cakes:
Gluten-Free Air Fryer Cod Filets:

Chapter Eleven: Tips and Tricks for Gluten-Free Air Fryer Cooking
Gluten-Free Flour and Breading Options:
Gluten-Free Sauce and Seasoning Ideas:
- Tomato sauce:
- BBQ sauce:
- Soy sauce:
- Hot Sauce:
- Pesto:
- Ranch dressing:

Spices:
How to adjust traditional recipes to be made in an air fryer
Troubleshooting Common Gluten-Free Air Fryer Problems:
The Versatility of Gluten-Free Air Fryer Cooking:

Introduction

Welcome to the world of deliciously crispy and flawlessly cooked gluten-free meals produced with the magic of the air fryer! If you enjoy the flavor and convenience of fried meals but must avoid gluten, you're in for a treat. Our gluten-free air fryer recipe book is coming to alter your culinary game, making it easier than ever to whip up delectable recipes that are safe and gratifying for your gluten-free lifestyle.

This exceptional treasure trove has a wealth of mouthwatering recipes that are sure to delight your taste buds. Everything from crunchy fried chicken and spicy onion rings to flavorful meatballs and beautiful french fries is gluten-free.

There are appetizer, entrée, side dish, and dessert recipes in this gluten-free air fryer recipe book. This recipe book for a gluten-free air fryer contains recipes like these

Crispy air-fried chicken tender

Sweet potato

Roasted vegetables

Air-fried salmon

Chocolate chip cookies

Gluten free sauce and seasoning idea

These dishes are all gluten-free and simple to cook in an air fryer, making them a practical and wholesome choice for those who have celiac disease or gluten allergies.

In addition to offering recipes, this gluten-free air fryer recipe book also offers guidance on how to pick the best air fryer, how to use one, and how to modify conventional recipes so they can be prepared in an air fryer.

Finally, this cookbook with gluten-free air fryer recipes is a helpful tool for anyone wishing to use an air fryer to prepare nutritious meals. You may simply make delicious and nourishing meals that satisfy your nutritional demands and fit into your busy lifestyle by selecting from a range of recipes.

Chapter One: Gluten-Free

About The Gluten Free

In recent years, the phrase "gluten-free" has gained popularity as more people, for a variety of reasons, have chosen to embrace a gluten-free diet. Wheat, barley, and rye all contain the protein gluten, which gives bread its elasticity and texture. However, ingesting gluten can have some harmful health repercussions for people who have celiac disease, gluten sensitivity, or a wheat allergy.

When gluten is ingested, the small intestine is attacked by the body's immune system, causing damage and inflammation. This condition is known as celiac disease. Contrarily, gluten sensitivity is a non-celiac disorder in which ingesting gluten might result in symptoms that are comparable to those of celiac disease without causing intestinal damage. In a different disorder known as wheat allergy, the immune system reacts to certain proteins in wheat, causing a variety of symptoms such as rashes, breathing problems, and digestive trouble.

A gluten-free diet must be followed for persons with these disorders to stay healthy. This entails staying away from all foods containing wheat, rye, barley, and any goods manufactured from these grains, such as pasta, bread, and cereals. Though many people think a gluten-free diet will result in better digestive health, more energy, and even weight loss, becoming gluten-free is not solely a choice made by those with illnesses linked to gluten.

Despite its widespread acceptance, eating a gluten-free diet has significant drawbacks. Eating out can be difficult for those who must avoid gluten, as many processed foods have hidden levels of protein. However, it is possible to live a successful gluten-free diet and take advantage of all its advantages with the correct information and tools.

Gluten-Free Air Fryer Cooking

Cooking in a gluten-free air fryer has gained popularity among people living gluten-free lifestyles. A small kitchen gadget known as an air fryer uses hot air to cook food fast and uniformly; it is comparable to a convection oven but is more portable. As the hot air produces a crispy coating without the need for deep frying, it's a great tool for people trying to make healthy meals with less oil.

Air fryers are an excellent choice for gluten-free cooking since they let you prepare a variety of foods without the danger of cross-contamination from gluten-containing goods. Many people who avoid gluten must exercise caution when using communal cooking areas or utensils since even minute levels of gluten can have negative health effects. With an air fryer, however, you can prepare gluten-free meals with confidence because you will know that no gluten will ever touch your food.

Additionally, highly adaptable air fryers let you prepare a huge variety of gluten-free foods. Without having to be concerned about cross-contamination, you may use them to make crispy chicken wings, french fries, and other fried dishes. Additionally, you can cook vegetables, fish, and other proteins in an air fryer to make delectable, wholesome meals that are risk-free for people with gluten sensitivities.

The fact that using an air fryer for gluten-free food is a quick and simple cooking method is another advantage. When compared to baking or frying food in an oven or on a stove, air fryers may cook food in a fraction of the time. This makes it a fantastic choice for people who are busy yet still want to prepare healthy meals at home without gluten.

In conclusion, folks wishing to prepare delectable, healthy, and secure meals have a lot of options, including cooking with a gluten-free air fryer. An air fryer can be a crucial appliance in any gluten-free kitchen because of its adaptability and speedy cooking times.

Science of Gluten-Free

The gluten protein is present in wheat, rye, and barley. It is in charge of giving bread and other baked goods their elastic texture and chewiness.

Consuming gluten can result in a number of unpleasant symptoms for those who have celiac disease or non-celiac gluten sensitivity, including lethargy, bloating, diarrhea, and abdominal pain.

Understanding how gluten interacts with the body and how to safely and successfully cut it out of the diet are both important aspects of the science behind gluten-free diets.

This necessitates a detailed awareness of laws governing food labeling, ingredient listings, and the availability of suitable gluten-free food alternatives.

A gluten-free diet may have health advantages even for those without celiac disease or gluten sensitivity, according to research.

According to several studies, avoiding gluten may improve gut health, immune system performance, and general health.

To completely comprehend the possible advantages and disadvantages of a gluten-free diet for the general population, more research is necessary.

Chapter Two: Basics of Gluten-Free Air Fryer Cooking

Foods free of the protein gluten, which is present in wheat, barley, and rye, can be prepared using the gluten-free air fryer technique. For those who have celiac disease or gluten sensitivity, gluten can cause gastrointestinal problems as well as other health complications.

You will require a gluten-free flour or flour blend before you can begin cooking with an air fryer. Rice flour, coconut flour, and almond flour are a few alternatives. A store-bought all-purpose flour mixture is another option. Due to the possibility of cross-contamination during the production process, it is crucial to ensure that the flour you use is gluten-free certified.

It's crucial to preheat your air fryer by the manufacturer's recommendations before using it to cook. The meal will cook more uniformly and to the proper degree of doneness as a result.

You can use a gluten-free flour mixture or gluten-free breading to cook gluten-free dishes in an air fryer. To aid in the air fryer's ability to crisp up the food, you can also apply a gluten-free cooking spray.

Foods devoid of gluten that cook well in an air fryer include:

Vegetables

Healthy and convenient air fryer vegetables include broccoli, cauliflower, and zucchini. Simple air-fried the vegetables till crispy after coating them in a gluten-free flour mixture.

Chicken

The air fryer can be used to prepare gluten-free breaded chicken tenders or nuggets. Just air-fried the chicken till crispy after coating it in a gluten-free flour mixture.
Potato wedges are cut into thin fries and dusted with a gluten-free flour combination. cook in the air till crisp and golden.

Fish:

An air fryer can be used to prepare gluten-free breaded fish. Simple air-fried the fish till crispy after coating it in a gluten-free flour mixture.

It's crucial to remember that not all foods will turn out nicely in an air fryer and that finding the ideal cooking times and temperatures for your specific appliance may require some trial and error. Always exercise caution when handling hot oil or items fried in the air fryer and always adhere to the manufacturer's directions.

Chapter Three: Choosing The Best Air Fryer

The ideal kitchen tool for giving you a healthier alternative to your favored fried foods is an air fryer. Choosing the best air fryer can be challenging with so many choices on the market. But don't fret! With these practical suggestions on how to pick the finest air fryer for your kitchen, we've got you covered.

Size Matters: Take into account the air fryer's size to ensure that it will suit your kitchen countertop and your cooking requirements. Different sized air fryers are available; they are usually sized in quarts. A compact air fryer with a lower capacity, such as 2-3 quarts, might be the best option if your kitchen is small or you have little counter room. However, you might require a larger air fryer with a greater capacity, such as 5-8 quarts, if you have a larger family or intend to cook larger portions.

Culinary Options: Select an air fryer with a wide range of culinary options. While air frying is the primary use, some air fryers also offer baking, grilling, and roasting options, making it a multipurpose household appliance. You can experiment with various recipes and broaden your palate by having multiple cooking functions.

Power and Temperature Control: Examine the air fryer's power and temperature control settings. If you want results sooner, choose an air fryer with a higher wattage because it will cook food more quickly. Additionally, temperature management is essential because it enables you to adjust the cooking temperature in accordance with your recipes.

For the best cooking versatility, look for an air fryer with a broad temperature range, typically between 180°F and 400°F.

Easy of Use: When choosing an air fryer, take user friendliness into account. Choose an air fryer with easy-to-use controls, a clear interface, and a legible monitor. Additionally, some air fryers have built-in cooking programs that can speed up and streamline the cooking process. A removable and dishwasher-safe basket or pan on an air fryer can also make cleanup simple.

Safety features: In any kitchen device, safety should always come first. For additional stability, search for air fryers with safety features like automatic shut-off, cool-touch handles, and non-slip feet. A safety lock feature is another feature that some air fryers have to avoid accidents or burns during cooking.

Brand Reputation and Reviews: To determine the reputation and dependability of the air fryer you are interested in, do some research on various companies and read customer reviews. Seek out companies with a solid reputation for creating high-quality appliances and happy customers. You can learn about the advantages and disadvantages of the air fryer by reading customer evaluations, which will aid in your decision-making.

Price and Warranty: Establish a spending limit for your air fryer and shop around for the best deals on various brands and types. While it may be tempting to choose the least expensive option, keep in mind that making a quality air fryer investment can pay off in the long term. Additionally, look into the manufacturer's warranty because it can give you peace of mind knowing that you are covered in the event that the appliance has any flaws or problems.

Choosing the best air fryer necessitates careful evaluation of a number of variables, including size, cooking functions, power and temperature control, ease of use, safety features, company reputation and reviews, price, and warranty. By considering these aspects, you can find the ideal air fryer that meets your requirements, improves your cooking, and enables you to indulge in healthier and delectable fried foods guilt-free. Have fun preparing!

Chapter Four: Breakfast Recipes

Whether you're following a gluten-free diet for medical reasons or personal preference, it can be challenging to find quick and easy breakfast options that fit your dietary needs. That's where the air fryer comes in. This handy kitchen appliance allows you to cook a variety of foods using minimal oil, making it a healthy and convenient option for breakfast.

In this collection, you'll find a range of delicious and satisfying gluten-free breakfast recipes that can be made in the air fryer. From savory breakfast sandwiches and breakfast burritos to sweet breakfast pastries and fruit, there's something for everyone. All of the recipes are easy to follow and can be made with simple, gluten-free ingredients that you can easily find at your local grocery store.
So why wait? Start your day off right with a tasty and healthy gluten-free breakfast made in the air fryer. Happy cooking!

Many delicious and easy gluten-free breakfast recipes can be made in an air fryer.

Below are a few ideas, let's get started!

Recipes:

Gluten-Free Air Fryer Omelet:

A gluten-free omelet made in an air fryer can be a quick and easy breakfast option for those following a gluten-free diet.

To make a gluten-free omelet in an air fryer, you will need a few ingredients and some basic kitchen equipment.

Ingredients:

2 eggs
2 tablespoons of milk or water
Salt and pepper, to taste
Your choices of gluten-free fillings, such as diced vegetables, cooked meat, or cheese

Equipment:

Air fryer
Small bowl
Whisk or fork
Spatula

Instructions:

- Preheat your air fryer to 360°F (190°C).

- Crack the eggs into a tiny bowl and beat them with a whisk or fork until they are well combined.

- Mix well after adding the milk or water to the eggs. Add salt and pepper to taste while seasoning the mixture.

- If using any fillings, such as diced vegetables or cooked meat, mix them into the egg mixture.

- Pour the egg mixture into the air fryer basket and smooth it out with a spatula.

- Place the basket into the preheated air fryer and cook for 8-10 minutes, or until the omelet is cooked through and the edges are crispy.

- Use a spatula to carefully remove the omelet from the air fryer basket and serve it immediately.

Enjoy your gluten-free omelet with your choices of sides, such as fruit, gluten-free toast, or a salad. This omelet is a quick and easy way to start your day with a protein-packed breakfast that is free of gluten.

Gluten-Free Air Fryer Pancakes:

Gluten-free air fryer pancakes are a tasty and convenient way to enjoy a classic breakfast dish without the use of wheat flour or other gluten-containing ingredients. They can be made using a variety of gluten-free flours, such as almond flour, coconut flour, or oat flour, and are cooked in an air fryer rather than on a stovetop griddle.

Ingredients:

1 cup gluten-free flour (almond flour, coconut flour, or oat flour work well)

1 teaspoon baking powder
1/2 teaspoon salt
1 cup milk (dairy or non-dairy)
1 egg
1 tablespoon melted butter or oil (optional)
1 teaspoon vanilla extract (optional)

Instructions

- Mix the gluten-free flour, baking powder, and salt in a large mixing bowl.

- In a different bowl, whisk together the milk, egg melted butter or oil, and vanilla extract.

- Pour the dry ingredients into the wet ingredients and stew until just incorporated.

- Preheat your air fryer to 370 F. Lightly coat the air fryer basket with cooking spray or a thin layer of oil.

- Drop spoonfuls of the pancake batter into the basket, leaving enough space between each pancake for them to expand.

- Cook the pancakes in the air fryer for 5-7 minutes, or until they are golden brown and cooked through.

- With your choice of toppings, such as butter, syrup, fruit, or whipped cream.

Serve the pancake hot

Overall, gluten-free air fryer pancakes are a delicious and convenient way to enjoy a classic breakfast dish without gluten.
They are very simple to make and can be customized with your favorite toppings. Give them a try and see for yourself!

Gluten-Free Air Fryer Breakfast Sandwich:

A gluten-free air fryer breakfast sandwich is a delicious and convenient way to start your day. You can easily customize the ingredients to suit your preferences and dietary needs. Here's how to make a gluten-free air fryer breakfast sandwich:

Ingredients:

2 slices of gluten-free bread
1 egg
1 slice of cheese (such as cheddar or Swiss)
2 slices of cooked bacon or sausage patties (optional)
Butter or non-stick cooking spray

Instructions:

- Preheat your air fryer to 360°F.

- Scatter butter or non-stick cooking spray on one side of each slice of bread.

- To lightly beat an egg, crack it into a small basin and use a fork.

- Put one slice of bread, butter side down, in the basket of the air fryer.

- Add the cheese slice, cooked bacon or sausage (if using), and scrambled egg as garnishes.

- Butter-side up, atop the first slice of bread, and place the second.

- Cook the sandwich in the air fryer for 5-7 minutes, or until the bread is toasted and the egg is cooked to your desired level of doneness.

- Carefully remove the sandwich from the air fryer and let it cool for a few minutes before serving.

Enjoy your gluten-free air fryer breakfast sandwich with a side of fruit or a cup of coffee for a satisfying and tasty start to your day.

Gluten-Free Sweet Potato Hash Browns:

To make gluten-free sweet potato hash browns in an air fryer, you will need the following ingredients:

2 medium sweet potatoes, peeled and grated
2 tablespoons of olive oil
Salt and pepper, to taste

Instructions:

- Preheat your fryer(the air fryer) to 390 degrees F.

- In a bowl, mix the grated sweet potatoes with olive oil, salt, and pepper.

- Place the sweet potato mixture in the air fryer basket, spreading it out in an even layer.

- Cook for 10-12 minutes, until the hash browns are crispy and golden brown.

Serve immediately and enjoy!

You can serve the hash browns with your choice of toppings, such as scrambled eggs, avocado, or diced tomatoes. They also taste great with a dollop of sour cream or Greek yogurt. Enjoy!

Gluten-Free Air Fryer Breakfast Potatoes:

Gluten-free air fryer breakfast potatoes are a delicious and healthy way to start your day.
They are easy to prepare and can be customized with your favorite seasonings and toppings.

Ingredients:

2 medium potatoes, washed and cut into small cubes

1 tablespoon olive oil

Salt and pepper, to taste

Any additional seasonings or toppings of your choice (such as herbs, spices, cheese, or vegetables)

Instructions:

- Preheat your air fryer to 400°F.

- In a small bowl, mix the cubed potatoes, olive oil, salt, and pepper.

- Place the potato mixture in the air fryer basket and cook for 15-20 minutes, shaking the basket occasionally, until the potatoes are tender and browned.

- Remove the potatoes from the air fryer and top them with any additional seasonings or toppings of your choice. Serve hot and enjoy!

These gluten-free air fryer breakfast potatoes are a quick and easy way to add some healthy and tasty variety to your breakfast routine.

They are also a great way to use up leftover potatoes and can be served alongside eggs, bacon, or other breakfast favorites.

Gluten-Free Air Fryer Granola Bars:

Here is a recipe for gluten-free granola bars that can be made in an air fryer:

Ingredients:

One cup of rolled oats (they must be certified gluten-free)
1/2 cup almond flour
1/2 cup sunflower seeds
1/2 cup pumpkin seeds
1/2 cup raisins
1/4 cup honey
1/4 cup almond butter
1 teaspoon vanilla extract
pinch of salt

Instructions:

- In a medium bowl, mix the oats, almond flour, sunflower seeds, pumpkin seeds, and raisins.

- In a separate small bowl, whisk together the honey, almond butter, vanilla extract, and salt.

- Pour the wet mixture over the dry mixture and stir until everything is well combined.

- Press the mixture firmly into an even layer at the bottom of the air fryer basket.

- Set the air fryer to 350°F and cook for 8-10 minutes, or until the edges of the granola bars are golden brown.

- Allow the granola bars to cool completely before cutting them into bars.

Enjoy!

Note: You may need to adjust the cooking time depending on the size and power of your air fryer.
Check on the granola bars frequently to make sure they are not burning.

Gluten-Free Air Fryer Breakfast Sausage Patties:

Here is a recipe for gluten-free air fryer breakfast sausage patties:

Ingredients:

1 pound ground pork
1/4 teaspoon salt
1/4 teaspoon black pepper
1/4 teaspoon garlic powder
1/4 teaspoon onion powder
1/4 teaspoon paprika

1/4 teaspoon dried thyme
1/4 teaspoon dried sage

Instructions:

- In a large bowl, mix the ground pork, salt, pepper, garlic powder, onion powder, paprika, thyme, and sage.

- Divide the mixture into four comparable quantities and form a patty with each quantity.

- Place the patties in the air fryer basket and set the temperature to 400°F.

- Cook the patties for 8-10 minutes, flipping halfway through, until they are cooked through and browned on both sides.

Serve the patties hot with your choice of accompaniments, such as eggs, toast, and fruit. Enjoy!

Note: If you don't have an air fryer, you can also cook these patties in a skillet over medium heat for about 6-8 minutes per side, or until they are cooked through and browned on both sides.

Gluten-Free Air Fryer Egg Muffins:

Gluten-free egg muffins are a quick and easy breakfast option that can be made in an air fryer. They are perfect for meal prep and can be made ahead of time and stored in the refrigerator or freezer for a quick and healthy breakfast option on busy mornings.

Ingredients:

8 large eggs
1/2 cup milk (dairy or non-dairy)
1/2 cup shredded cheese (optional)
1/4 cup diced vegetables (such as bell peppers, onions, and spinach)
Salt and pepper, to taste

Instructions:

- Preheat your air fryer to 350°F.

- Prepare a large mixing bowl and whisk the eggs with the milk until well combined.

- Stir in the diced vegetables and cheese, if using. Season with salt and pepper.

- Lightly coat a muffin tin with cooking spray. Turn the egg mixture evenly into the muffin cups, filling them about 3/4 full.

- Place the muffin tin in the air fryer and cook for 12-15 minutes, or until the eggs are set and the muffins are lightly golden on top.

- Remove the muffin tin from the air fryer and let the muffins cool for a few minutes before serving.
  They can be stored in an airtight container in the refrigerator for up to 5 days or in the freezer for up to 3 months.

Enjoy your gluten-free egg muffins as a quick and easy breakfast on the go or as a protein-packed snack. You can customize them with your favorite vegetables and cheese for added flavor and nutrition.

Gluten-Free Air Fryer Breakfast Quiche:

A gluten-free air fryer quiche makes a delicious and satisfying breakfast option for those who follow a gluten-free diet or have celiac disease. The following basic ingredients are required to produce this recipe:

Eggs:
You will need a few eggs to create the base of the quiche. You can use whole eggs or just egg whites, depending on your preference and dietary needs.

Gluten-free flour:
You will need gluten-free flour to create the crust of the quiche. There are many different types of gluten-free flour available, such as almond flour, coconut flour, and rice flour.

Milk:
You will need a small amount of milk to help create a creamy texture in the quiche. You can use any type of milk, such as cow's milk, almond milk, or soy milk.

Filling ingredients:

You can add a variety of ingredients to the quiche to customize the flavor and texture. Some options include diced vegetables, diced ham, bacon, cheese, and herbs.

Instructions

- start by mixing the eggs, gluten-free flour, and milk in a bowl.
- add in your desired filling ingredients and mix well.
- Pour the mixture into a pie dish or quiche pan and place it in the air fryer.
- Cook the quiche at 350 degrees Fahrenheit for about 20-25 minutes, or until the center is set and the crust is golden brown.

Serve the quiche hot, garnished with fresh herbs or a sprinkle of cheese if desired.

This gluten-free quiche is perfect for a leisurely weekend breakfast or as a quick and easy breakfast option during the week. Enjoy!

Gluten-Free Air Fryer Bacon:

Gluten-free air fryer bacon is a delicious and easy-to-make snack or breakfast option that is suitable for those who follow a gluten-free diet.

Ingredients:

Bacon slices (make sure they are labeled as gluten-free)

Instructions:

- Preheat your fryer(air fryer) to 390 F.

- Place the bacon slices in the basket of the air fryer, making sure not to overlap the slices.

- Cook the bacon for about 8-12 minutes, depending on the thickness of the slices and your desired level of crispiness.

- Check the bacon frequently and flip the slices over halfway through cooking to ensure even cooking.

- Once the bacon is cooked to your desired level of crispiness, remove it from the air fryer and place it on a paper towel-lined plate to drain any excess grease.

- Serve the bacon hot and enjoy!

One of the benefits of cooking bacon in an air fryer is that it can be done quickly and with less mess than cooking it in a pan on the stove. Additionally, because the bacon is cooked in the basket of the air fryer, the excess grease is drained away, making it a healthier option compared to traditional pan-fried bacon.

As always, it is important to double-check the ingredient list of any products you use to ensure they are gluten-free.

Some brands of bacon may use gluten-containing ingredients in their curing process, so be sure to choose a brand that specifically states that their bacon is gluten-free.

Gluten-Free Air Fryer French Toast:

To make gluten-free French toast in an air fryer, you will need:

Ingredients:

4 slices of gluten-free bread
2 eggs
1/2 cup milk (dairy or non-dairy)
1 teaspoon vanilla extract
1/2 teaspoon cinnamon
A pinch of salt
Butter or oil, for lubricating the fryer basket
Maple syrup and sugar powder, for serving if desired.

Instructions:

- Preheat your air fryer to 390°F (200°C).

- In a shallow dish, beat together the eggs, milk, vanilla extract, cinnamon, and salt.

- Scoop each slice of bread into the egg combination, coating both sides evenly.

- Lightly grease the fryer basket with oil

- Position the coated bread slices in the basket, making sure not to overcrowd them.

- Cook the French toast for about 6-8 minutes, flipping halfway through, until golden brown and crispy. If your air fryer has a "toast" setting, you can use that as well.

- Serve the French toast hot, topped with maple syrup and a dusting of powdered sugar, if desired. Enjoy!

Note: You can also add your favorite toppings, such as fruit, whipped cream, or nut butter, to customize your gluten-free French toast.

Just be sure to use gluten-free ingredients to ensure that the dish is safe for those with gluten sensitivities or allergies.

Chapter Five: Snacks and Appetizers

Some many delicious gluten-free snacks and appetizers can be made in an air fryer.

Recipes:

Gluten-Free Air Fryer Mozzarella Sticks:

Gluten-free air fryer mozzarella sticks are a delicious and convenient snack or appetizer that can be made using an air fryer and gluten-free ingredients. They are a great option for those who are following a gluten-free diet or are allergic to gluten.

To make gluten-free mozzarella sticks, you will need:

Gluten-free flour:
This can be made by mixing a combination of gluten-free flour, such as almond flour, chickpea flour, and tapioca flour.

Egg:
This will be used to coat the mozzarella sticks and help the gluten-free flour stick to them.

Panko breadcrumbs:
These are made from gluten-free bread and can be found at most grocery stores or online.

Mozzarella cheese:

Look for mozzarella cheese sticks that are made with gluten-free ingredients.

Instructions

- Cut the mozzarella cheese into long, thin sticks.

- Whisk an egg in a tiny bowl and set aside.

- In a separate bowl, mix the gluten-free flour and panko breadcrumbs.

- Dip each mozzarella stick into the egg, then coat it with the gluten-free flour mixture, making sure to evenly coat it on all sides.

- Preheat your fryer(air fryer) to 390 F.

- Place the coated mozzarella sticks in the air fryer basket, making sure to leave some space between them.

- Cook for about 5-6 minutes, or until the mozzarella sticks are golden brown and the cheese is melted.

Serve the mozzarella sticks hot, with your choice of dipping sauce. They are delicious on their own, but you can also serve them with marinara sauce, ranch dressing, or any other sauce that you enjoy.

Overall, gluten-free air fryer mozzarella sticks are a tasty and easy-to-make snack or appetizer that can be enjoyed by anyone, regardless of their dietary restrictions. Try them and see them for yourself!

Gluten-Free Air Fryer Buffalo Wings:

Here is a recipe for gluten-free buffalo wings made in an air fryer:

Ingredients:

1 pound chicken wings
2 tablespoons olive oil
1 teaspoon garlic powder
1 teaspoon onion powder
1 teaspoon paprika
1/2 teaspoon salt
1/2 cup gluten-free hot sauce (such as Frank's RedHot)
1 tablespoon unsalted butter, melted

Instructions:

- Preheat your air fryer to 390°F.

- In a small bowl, mix the olive oil, garlic powder, onion powder, paprika, and salt.

- Place the chicken wings in a large bowl and coat them with the spice mixture.

- Cook the chicken wings in the air fryer basket for 16 minutes.

- In a separate small bowl, mix the hot sauce and melted butter.

- After 15 minutes, remove the chicken wings from the air fryer and brush them with the hot sauce mixture.

- Return the wings to the air fryer and cook for an additional 5-10 minutes, until the wings are cooked through and the sauce is caramelized.

- Serve the wings with your favorite dipping sauce, such as ranch or blue cheese dressing. Enjoy!

Note: If you don't have an air fryer, you can also bake the wings in the oven. Preheat the oven to 400°F and bake the wings for 20-25 minutes, until they are cooked through. Brush with the hot sauce mixture and bake for an additional 5-10 minutes, until the sauce is caramelized.

Gluten-Free Air Fryer Jalapeno Poppers:

Gluten-free air fryer jalapeno poppers are a tasty and convenient snack or appetizer that can be easily prepared in an air fryer.

Ingredients:

6 jalapeno peppers
6 ounces of cream cheese, softened
1/2 cup shredded cheddar cheese
1/4 cup chopped bacon

1/4 cup diced onion
1/4 cup diced bell pepper
1 clove of garlic, minced
1/4 teaspoon salt
1/4 teaspoon black pepper
1/4 teaspoon cumin
1/4 cup gluten-free breadcrumbs

Instructions:

- Remove the seeds and veins from the jalapeño peppers by cutting them in half lengthwise.

- In a small bowl, mix the cream cheese, cheddar cheese, bacon, onion, bell pepper, garlic, salt, pepper, and cumin.

- Fill the jalapeno pepper halves with the cheese mixture.

- In a separate bowl, mix the breadcrumbs with a little bit of oil or melted butter.

- Roll the stuffed jalapeno peppers in the breadcrumbs to coat them evenly.

- Place the jalapeno poppers in the air fryer basket, making sure they are not overcrowded.

- Set the air fryer to 400°F and cook the poppers for 10-12 minutes, or until they are golden brown and the cheese is melted and bubbly.

- Serve the jalapeno poppers hot, with your favorite dipping sauce, or as a stand-alone snack.

You can also customize these jalapeno poppers by adding your favorite ingredients to the cheese mixture, such as diced ham, crumbled sausage, or chopped herbs. Enjoy!

Gluten-Free Air Fryer Pickles:

Pickles are a great snack to make in an air fryer because they cook quickly and come out crispy. To make gluten-free pickles in an air fryer, you will need:

Ingredients:

1 jar of pickles (make sure they are gluten-free)
1 cup of gluten-free breadcrumbs
1 egg
1 tsp garlic powder
1 tsp onion powder
1 tsp paprika

Instructions:

- Preheat your air fryer to 400°F.

- In a shallow dish, beat the egg.

- In a separate shallow dish, mix the breadcrumbs, garlic powder, onion powder, and paprika.

- Dip each pickle slice into the egg, making sure to coat both sides.

- Transfer the pickles to the breadcrumb mixture and coat evenly.

- Place the breaded pickles in the air fryer basket in a single layer.

- Cook the pickles for 5-7 minutes, until they are crispy and golden brown.

Remove the pickles from the air fryer and let them cool for a few minutes before serving.

Enjoy your crispy and delicious gluten-free air fryer pickles!

Gluten-Free Air Fryer Plantain Chips:

Plantain chips are a delicious and healthy snack option that can be easily made in an air fryer.
They are naturally gluten-free, making them suitable for people with gluten sensitivities or celiac disease.

To make gluten-free plantain chips in an air fryer, you will need:

1 or 2 ripe plantains
Olive oil or coconut oil spray
Salt (optional)

Instructions:

- Preheat your air fryer to 400°F (200°C).

- Slice the plantains into thin rounds, about 1/8 inch thick.

- Spray the plantain slices with a light coating of olive oil or coconut oil.

- Place the plantain slices in a single layer in the air fryer basket.

- If desired, sprinkle the plantain slices with a little bit of salt.

- Air fry the plantain chips for about 8-10 minutes until they are crispy and golden brown.

- Remove the plantain chips from the air fryer and let them cool for a few minutes before serving.

Enjoy your gluten-free plantain chips as a snack on their own, or serve them with your favorite dip or salsa. They are a tasty and healthy alternative to traditional potato chips and are sure to be a hit with everyone in your household.

Gluten-Free Air Fryer Falafel:

Gluten-free falafel can be made in an air fryer and is a delicious and healthy alternative to traditional falafel, which is typically made with wheat-based flour.

Ingredients:

One cup of dried chickpeas, soaked in water all night and drained
1 small onion, finely chopped
3 cloves garlic, minced
1/4 cup chopped fresh parsley
1/4 cup chopped fresh cilantro
1 teaspoon ground cumin
1 teaspoon ground coriander
1/2 teaspoon ground chili flakes
1/2 teaspoon salt
1/4 teaspoon ground black pepper
2 tablespoons chickpea flour
1 tablespoon olive oil

Instructions

- Place the soaked and drained chickpeas, onion, garlic, parsley, cilantro, cumin, coriander, chili flakes, salt, and pepper in a food processor.

- Pulse the mixture until it is well combined and resembles a coarse paste. Stir in the chickpea flour and olive oil.

- Use your hands to shape the falafel mixture into small balls, about the size of a golf ball.

- Place the balls on a plate and refrigerate for at least 30 minutes to allow them to firm up.

- Preheat your air fryer to 390°F (200°C).

- Place the falafel balls in the air fryer basket and cook for 10-12 minutes, or until they are golden brown and crisp.

- Serve the falafel hot, with your choice of dipping sauce or garnishes. Enjoy!

Gluten-Free Air Fryer Broccoli Bites:

Gluten-free air fryer broccoli bites are a delicious and healthy snack that can be easily made at home.

These are what you will need to make this bites:

Ingredients:

Cut one head of broccoli into bite-sized florets
1 cup of gluten-free breadcrumbs
1 egg, beaten
1/4 cup of grated Parmesan cheese

Salt and pepper to taste
Olive oil spray

Instructions:

- Preheat your fryer(air fryer) to 390 F.

- In a small bowl, beat the egg. In a separate bowl, mix the breadcrumbs, Parmesan cheese, salt, and pepper.

- Dip the broccoli florets into the egg, then roll them in the breadcrumb mixture until they are evenly coated.

- Place the coated broccoli florets in the air fryer basket, being sure to not overcrowd the basket.

- Lightly spray the florets with olive oil.

- Cook the broccoli bites for 10-12 minutes, or until they are golden brown and crispy.

- Extract the bites from the air fryer and serve them hot.

These gluten-free broccoli bites are a great snack or appetizer that can be served on their own or with a dipping sauce of your choice.
They are also a great way to get your daily serving of vegetables while still indulging in a tasty treat. Enjoy!

Gluten-Free Air Fryer Onion Rings:

Gluten-free onion rings can be made in an air fryer with just a few simple ingredients and steps. Here is a recipe for gluten-free onion rings that you can make in your air fryer:

Ingredients:

1 large onion, thinly sliced into rings
1 cup gluten-free flour (such as almond flour or coconut flour)
1 teaspoon garlic powder
1 teaspoon onion powder
1 teaspoon paprika
1/2 teaspoon salt
1 cup water
1 egg, beaten
1 cup gluten-free breadcrumbs
Oil for spraying (optional)

Instructions:

- Preheat your air fryer to 400°F.

- In a shallow dish, mix the gluten-free flour, garlic powder, onion powder, paprika, and salt.

- In a different shallow dish, whip the egg with the water.

- Place the gluten-free breadcrumbs in a third shallow dish.

- Dip the onion rings into the flour mixture, then into the egg mixture, and finally into the breadcrumbs, making sure they are well coated with each.

- Place the coated onion rings into the basket of the air fryer in a single layer, being sure not to overcrowd the basket.

- If desired, lightly spray the onion rings with oil.

- Cook the onion rings in the air fryer for 8-10 minutes, or until they are golden brown and crispy.

- Serve the gluten-free onion rings immediately, with your choice of dipping sauce.

Enjoy your delicious gluten-free onion rings!

Gluten-Free Air Fryer Avocado Fries:

Avocado fries are a delectable and healthy option to traditional fried foods.
They can be made in an air fryer, which uses hot air to cook the food, resulting in a crispy exterior and a tender interior.

Ingredients:

2 ripe avocados
1 cup almond flour

1 teaspoon garlic powder
1 teaspoon onion powder
1 teaspoon chili powder
1 teaspoon salt
2 eggs, beaten
Olive oil cooking spray

Instructions

- Preheat your air fryer to 400°F.
- Cut the avocados into 1/2-inch slices.
- In a shallow bowl, mix the almond flour, garlic powder, onion powder, chili powder, and salt.
- Dip each avocado slice into the beaten eggs, then coat with the almond flour mixture.
- Place the coated avocado slices in the air fryer basket, making sure they are not touching.
- Lightly spray the avocado slices with olive oil cooking spray.
- Cook the avocado slices in the air fryer for 8-10 minutes, or until they are golden brown and crispy.
- Remove the avocado fries from the air fryer and serve immediately with your favorite dipping sauce.

These gluten-free avocado fries are a tasty and healthy snack that the whole family will love. Enjoy!

Chapter Six: Main Courses

Many delicious main course options can be made in an air fryer that is also gluten-free. Some ideas include:
No matter what main course you choose, be sure to use a gluten-free flour or coating mixture to ensure that your dish is completely gluten-free.

Recipes:

Gluten-Free Air Fryer Fried Chicken:

Here is a recipe for gluten-free air fryer fried chicken:

Ingredients:

A pound of skinless, boneless chicken thighs or breasts.
1 cup gluten-free flour (such as almond flour or coconut flour)
2 teaspoons paprika
1 teaspoon garlic powder
1 teaspoon onion powder
1 teaspoon salt
1/2 teaspoon black pepper
2 large eggs
2 tablespoons water

Instructions:

- Preheat your air fryer to 400°F.

- In a shallow dish, mix the gluten-free flour, paprika, garlic powder, onion powder, salt, and black pepper.

- In a separate shallow dish, whisk together the eggs and water.

- Dip each piece of chicken into the egg mixture, making sure to coat it evenly, then transfer it to the dish with the flour mixture.

- Coat the chicken evenly with the flour mixture, pressing it firmly into the chicken to make sure it sticks.

- Place the coated chicken in the air fryer basket in a single layer, leaving a little bit of space between each piece.

- Cook the chicken for 8-10 minutes, flipping it halfway through until it is cooked through and the outside is crispy and golden.

- Take out the chicken from the air fryer and let it rest for some minutes before serving.

Enjoy!

Gluten-Free Air Fryer Steak Fajitas:

Gluten-free steak fajitas made in an air fryer are a delicious and healthy option for those following a gluten-free diet or looking for a quick and easy dinner idea.

Ingredients:

1 pound of thinly sliced steak (sirloin or flank steak work well)
1 red bell pepper, thinly sliced
1 yellow bell pepper, thinly sliced
1 green bell pepper, thinly sliced
1 onion, thinly sliced
2 cloves of garlic, minced
2 tablespoons of olive oil
1 teaspoon of chili powder
1 teaspoon of cumin
1 teaspoon of paprika
Salt and pepper to taste

Instructions

- Start by mixing the chili powder, cumin, paprika, salt, and pepper in a small bowl.

- Rub the spice mixture onto both sides of the steak slices.

- heat the air fryer to 400°F.

- Place the steak slices into the air fryer basket and cook for 6-8 minutes, flipping halfway through, until the steak is cooked to your desired level of doneness.

- Take out the steak from the air fryer and put it aside.

- While the steak is cooking, heat the olive oil in a large skillet over medium heat.

- Add the sliced peppers, onion, and minced garlic to the skillet and sauté until the vegetables are tender.

- Once the vegetables are cooked, slice the steak into thin strips and add it to the skillet with the vegetables.

- Stir everything together to combine.

Serve the steak fajitas with your choice of gluten-free tortillas or over a bed of rice. Top with your favorite fajita toppings, such as guacamole, salsa, and shredded cheese. Enjoy!

Gluten-Free Air Fryer Shrimp Scampi:

Gluten-free shrimp scampi is a delicious and easy-to-prepare meal that can be made in an air fryer.

It's a great option for those following a gluten-free diet or for anyone looking for a healthier alternative to traditional fried shrimp.

Ingredients

1 pound of large, peeled, and deveined shrimp
2 tablespoons of olive oil
2 cloves of minced garlic
2 tablespoons of lemon juice
1/2 teaspoon of salt
1/4 teaspoon of black pepper
1/4 teaspoon of red pepper flakes (optional)
2 tablespoons of chopped fresh parsley

Instructions

- Mix the olive oil, garlic, lemon juice, salt, black pepper, and red pepper flakes (if using) in a small bowl.

- Place the shrimp in a large bowl and pour the marinade over them, tossing to coat the shrimp evenly.

- Preheat your fryer(air fryer) to 390 F.

- Place the shrimp in the basket of the air fryer in a single layer, making sure not to overcrowd the basket.

- Cook the shrimp for 6-8 minutes, flipping halfway through until they are pink and cooked through.

- Sprinkle the chopped parsley over the cooked shrimp and serve immediately.

Enjoy your gluten-free shrimp scampi with a side of your favorite vegetables or a salad. It's a tasty and healthy meal that the whole family will love!

Gluten-Free Air Fryer Brussels Sprouts:

Here is a recipe for gluten-free air fryer Brussels sprouts:

Ingredients:

1 pound Brussels sprouts, trimmed and halved
1 tablespoon olive oil
1/4 teaspoon salt
1/4 teaspoon black pepper

Instructions:

- Preheat your air fryer to 400°F (200°C).

- In a portable bowl, mix the salt, pepper, and olive oil.

- Set the Brussels sprouts in a single layer in the fryer basket. Brush with the olive oil mixture.

- Cook the Brussels sprouts for 10-12 minutes, or until they are tender and caramelized.

- Shake the basket halfway through to ensure actual cooking.

- Serve the Brussels sprouts immediately, garnished with additional salt and pepper if desired.

These gluten-free air fryer Brussels sprouts make a delicious and healthy side dish that can be served with a variety of main courses. They are easy to prepare and cook quickly in the air fryer, making them a convenient option for busy weeknights. Enjoy!

Gluten-Free Air Fryer Tofu Skewers:

Here is a recipe for gluten-free air fryer tofu skewers:

Ingredients:

One block of firm extra-firm tofu
1/4 cup of gluten-free soy sauce
1 tablespoon of honey
1 tablespoon of rice vinegar
1 clove of garlic, minced
1/2 teaspoon of grated ginger
1/2 teaspoon of sesame oil
Wooden skewers damped in water for at least 40 minutes
Sesame seeds, for garnishment (optional)

Instructions:

- Press the tofu for at least 15 minutes to remove excess moisture. You can do this by placing the tofu between two paper towels or a clean dish towel and pressing it down with a heavy object, such as a cast iron pan or a cutting board.

- Cut the tofu into 1-inch cubes and set aside.

- In a small bowl, mix the soy sauce, honey, rice vinegar, minced garlic, grated ginger, and sesame oil.

- Place the tofu cubes in a shallow dish or zip-top bag and pour the marinade over them. Let the tofu marinate for at least 30 minutes or up to 2 hours.

- Preheat the air fryer to 400°F.

- Thread the marinated tofu onto the soaked skewers, making sure to leave a little bit of space between each piece.

- Set the skewers in the fryer basket, do not let them touch.

- Cook the tofu skewers for 10-12 minutes, turning halfway through until the tofu is crispy and browned.

- If you want, garnish with sesame seeds and serve immediately.

These tofu skewers are delicious and served with a side of rice and your favorite vegetables. You can also serve them as an appetizer or as part of a larger meal. Enjoy!

Gluten-Free Air Fryer Salmon Filets:

Here is a recipe for gluten-free air fryer salmon filets:

Ingredients:

2 salmon filets
1 teaspoon olive oil
Salt and pepper, to taste
2 tablespoons gluten-free breadcrumbs (such as almond flour or coconut flour)
1/2 teaspoon paprika
1/2 teaspoon garlic powder
1/2 teaspoon onion powder

Instructions:

- Preheat your air fryer to 390°F.

- Use olive oil to brush the salmon filets and season with pepper and salt.

- In a small bowl, mix the gluten-free breadcrumbs, paprika, garlic powder, and onion powder.

- Coat the salmon filets in the breadcrumb mixture, pressing gently to help it adhere.

- Place the salmon filets in the air fryer basket and cook for 10-12 minutes, or until the internal temperature reaches 145°F.

- Serve the salmon filets hot, with your choice of sides and sauces.

Tips:

You can also add a squeeze of lemon juice or a sprinkle of fresh herbs (such as parsley or dill) to the breadcrumb mixture for extra flavor.

I hope you enjoy this recipe!

Chapter Seven: Sides and Vegetable Dishes

Here are some ideas for gluten-free air fryer side dishes and vegetable dishes:

Recipes:

Gluten-Free Air Fryer Roasted Vegetables:

Ingredients:

2 cups of vegetables (such as bell peppers, zucchini, and onions)
2 tablespoons of olive oil
1 teaspoon of salt
1/2 teaspoon of black pepper
1/2 teaspoon of garlic powder
1/2 teaspoon of dried basil

Instructions:

- Preheat your air fryer to 400°F.

- Cut the vegetables into small, evenly sized pieces.

- In a small bowl, mix the olive oil, salt, black pepper, garlic powder, and dried basil.

- Place the vegetables in a large bowl and toss with the oil and spice mixture until they are evenly coated.

- Place the vegetables in the air fryer basket in a single layer, making sure not to overcrowd the basket.

- Cook the vegetables for 10-12 minutes, or until they are tender and lightly browned.

- Serve the roasted vegetables hot, garnished with additional salt and pepper if desired.

Note: You can use any vegetables you like for this recipe. Some other options include carrots, broccoli, and mushrooms. Just make sure to cut them into small pieces so they cook evenly in the air fryer.

Gluten-Free Sweet Potato Fries:

Here is a recipe for gluten-free sweet potato fries made in an air fryer:

Ingredients:

Three portable sweet potatoes, peeled and trim into thin wedges
2 tablespoons olive oil
1 teaspoon paprika
1/2 teaspoon garlic powder
1/2 teaspoon onion powder
1/4 teaspoon salt
Optional: 1/4 teaspoon black pepper

Instructions:

- Preheat your air fryer to 400°F.

- In a tiny bowl, blend the paprika, garlic powder, onion powder, salt, and black pepper (if using).

- Place the sweet potato wedges in a large bowl and drizzle with the olive oil.

- Sprinkle the seasoning mixture over the top and toss to coat the wedges evenly.

- Place the sweet potato wedges in the air fryer basket in a single layer.

- Cook for 10 minutes, then flip the wedges and cook for an additional 5-10 minutes, or until they are tender and golden brown.

- Serve the sweet potato fries immediately, with your choice of dipping sauce if desired.

Enjoy!

These sweet potato fries are a healthy and delicious alternative to regular french fries, and the air fryer makes them crispy on the outside and tender on the inside. Just be sure to use a gluten-free seasoning mixture to ensure that the recipe is safe for those with gluten sensitivities or celiac disease.

Gluten-Free Air Fryer Zucchini Chips:

If you're following a gluten-free diet or are sensitive to gluten, finding tasty snack options can be a challenge. Luckily, these gluten-free air fryer zucchini chips are a delicious and convenient option that everyone can enjoy.

Ingredients:

1 medium zucchini, sliced into thin rounds
1 egg, beaten
1/2 cup gluten-free breadcrumbs
1/4 cup grated Parmesan cheese
Salt and pepper, to taste

Instructions:

- Preheat your air fryer to 400°F.

- Prepare a shallow dish and combine the Parmesan cheese and breadcrumbs

- Dip the zucchini slices in the beaten egg, then coat with the breadcrumb mixture.

- Place the coated zucchini slices in a single layer in the air fryer basket.

- Sprinkle it with salt and pepper.

- Cook for 8-10 minutes, until the zucchini chips are golden brown and crispy.

- Withdraw from the fryer and serve instantly.

These gluten-free zucchini chips are a great snack for those following a gluten-free diet, as well as for anyone looking for a healthier alternative to fried snacks.

They are crispy on the outside and tender on the inside, and the combination of breadcrumbs and Parmesan cheese gives them a delicious flavor.

Enjoy them on their own, or serve them with your favorite dipping sauce.

Gluten-Free Air Fryer Fried Green Potatoes:

Fried green potatoes are a tasty and satisfying side dish that can be easily made in an air fryer.

To make gluten-free fried green potatoes, you'll need a few simple ingredients:

Ingredients:

Green potatoes (unripe or slightly under-ripe potatoes work best for this recipe)
Gluten-free flour (coconut flour or almond flour)
Salt
Pepper
Olive oil or cooking spray

Instructions:

- Wash and slice the green potatoes into thin wedges or rounds.

- In a shallow dish, mix the gluten-free flour, salt, and pepper.

- Coat the potato slices in the flour mixture, shaking off any excess.

- Preheat the air fryer to 390°F.

- Place the coated potato slices in the air fryer basket in a single layer, making sure not to overcrowd the basket.

- Lightly spray the potatoes with olive oil or cooking spray.

- Cook the potatoes in the air fryer for 8-10 minutes, or until they are crispy and golden brown. Flip the potatoes halfway through cooking to ensure even browning.

Serve the fried green potatoes hot, with your choice of dipping sauce or as a side dish. Enjoy!

Gluten-Free Air Fryer Grilled Corn on the Cob:

Grilled corn on the cob is a classic summertime treat, and it's easy to make in an air fryer if you're following a gluten-free diet.

Instructions

- Preheat your air fryer to 390°F.

- While the air fryer is heating up, prepare your corn on the cob by removing the husks and silks.

- Some people like to soak their corn in water for a few minutes before grilling to help prevent it from drying out, but this step is optional.

- Set the corn on the cob in the air fryer basket, making sure not to overcrowd it.
  You may need to work in batches if you have a lot of corn.

- Cook the corn for about 15-20 minutes, or until it reaches your desired level of tenderness. You may need to rotate the corn halfway through cooking to ensure even cooking.

- Once the corn is cooked, remove it from the air fryer and let it cool for a few minutes.

- Then, you can add any desired toppings, such as butter, salt, and pepper.

Enjoy your gluten-free grilled corn on the cob!

Gluten-Free Air Fryer Asparagus:

Asparagus is a delicious and nutritious vegetable that is naturally gluten-free. It is a great choice for people following a gluten-free diet, and it can be easily cooked in an air fryer. Here's a simple recipe for gluten-free air fryer asparagus:

Ingredients:

1 bunch of asparagus, ends trimmed
1 tablespoon olive oil
Salt and pepper, to taste

Instructions:

- Preheat your air fryer to 390°F

- Put the asparagus in a bowl and mist with olive oil.

- Spice up with salt and pepper to taste.

- Set the asparagus in the fryer basket in a single layer.

- Cook the asparagus for 8-10 minutes, shaking the basket halfway through cooking. The asparagus is ready when it is tender and has a slight char on the edges.

Serve the asparagus hot, garnished with additional salt and pepper, if desired.

This recipe is quick, easy, and flavorful, and it makes a great side dish for any meal. If you prefer more crispy asparagus, you can increase the cooking time by a few minutes. Just be sure to keep an eye on it to avoid burning. Enjoy!

Gluten-Free Air Fryer Artichokes:

Cooking artichokes in an air fryer is a quick and easy way to prepare this tasty vegetable.
To make gluten-free air fryer artichokes, you will need:

Ingredients:

2 large artichokes
1 lemon, sliced
2 cloves of garlic, minced
2 tablespoons olive oil
Salt and pepper to taste

Instructions:

- Rinse the artichokes under cold water and cut off the stem so that they can stand upright.

- Using kitchen scissors, snip off the sharp tips of the leaves.

- Place the artichokes in a large bowl and squeeze the lemon slices over them.

- Add the minced garlic and toss to coat the artichokes.

- Drizzle the olive oil over the artichokes and season with salt and pepper.

- Preheat your air fryer to 400°F (200°C).

- Place the artichokes in the air fryer basket and cook for 20-25 minutes, or until the leaves are tender and the outer layers are golden brown.

- Serve the artichokes hot, with your choice of dipping sauces.

Some options include melted butter, mayonnaise, or a vegan aioli. Enjoy!

Note: If you prefer your artichokes more tender, you can steam them for about 10 minutes before placing them in the air fryer.
This will help to soften the leaves and make them easier to pull off and eat.

Gluten-Free Air Fryer Peppers:

Ingredients:

1 pound bell peppers, sliced into 1/4 inch strips
2 tablespoons olive oil
1/2 teaspoon salt
1/4 teaspoon black pepper
1/4 teaspoon garlic powder

Instructions:

- Preheat your air fryer to 390°F.

- In a small bowl, mix the olive oil, salt, black pepper, and garlic powder.

- Place the sliced peppers in a single layer in the air fryer basket.

- Brush the peppers with the olive oil mixture, making sure to coat them evenly.

- Place the basket in the air fryer and cook for 8-10 minutes, or until the peppers are tender and slightly charred.

- Serve the peppers immediately as a side dish or topping for salads, sandwiches, or bowls. Enjoy!

Note: If you are sensitive to gluten, make sure to use a gluten-free olive oil and check the labels of any other ingredients you use to ensure they are gluten-free as well.

Gluten-Free Air Fryer Mushrooms:

Air fryer mushrooms are a quick and easy snack or side dish that can be made gluten-free by using gluten-free ingredients.

Ingredients:

8 ounces mushrooms (such as cremini, white button, or shiitake)
1 tablespoon olive oil
1/2 teaspoon garlic powder
1/2 teaspoon onion powder
1/4 teaspoon salt
1/4 teaspoon black pepper

Instructions:

- Preheat your fryer to 390°F.

- In a small bowl, mix the olive oil, garlic powder, onion powder, salt, and pepper.

- Place the mushrooms in a single layer in the basket of the air fryer.

- Use olive oil mixture to brush the mushrooms.

- Air fry the mushrooms for 8-10 minutes until they are tender and browned.

- Remove the mushrooms from the air fryer and serve immediately.

Optional: You can add other seasonings to the olive oil mixture, such as Italian seasoning, paprika, or dried herbs, to give the mushrooms extra flavor.

You can also sprinkle the mushrooms with grated parmesan cheese before air frying for an extra cheesy twist. Enjoy!

Gluten-Free Air Fryer Green Beans:

Here is a recipe for gluten-free air fryer green beans:

Ingredients:

1 pound fresh green beans, trimmed
1 tablespoon olive oil
Salt and pepper, to taste

Instructions:

- Preheat your air fryer to 390°F.

- In a tiny bowl, toss the green beans with olive oil and a pinch of salt and pepper.

- Place the green beans in the air fryer basket in a single layer, making sure not to overcrowd the basket.

- Air fry the green beans for 8-10 minutes, shaking the basket halfway through until they are tender and crispy.

Serve the green beans desirable and enjoy!

You can also add additional seasonings to the green beans, such as garlic powder or Italian seasoning, to give them a little extra flavor.
If you prefer a softer texture, you can reduce the cooking time slightly.
Just be sure to keep an eye on the green beans as they cook to avoid burning them.

Gluten-Free Air Fryer Eggplant:

Eggplant is a delicious and versatile vegetable that can be cooked in a variety of ways, including in an air fryer.
If you are following a gluten-free diet, you'll be happy to know that eggplant is naturally gluten-free, so you can easily incorporate it into your meals.

Ingredients:

1 medium eggplant, sliced into 1/4-inch rounds
2 tablespoons olive oil

1/2 teaspoon salt

1/4 teaspoon black pepper

Instructions:

- Preheat your fryer to 390°F.

- In a portable bowl, mix the olive oil, salt, and pepper.

- Place the eggplant slices in a single layer in the basket of the air fryer.

- Use the olive oil mixture to brush the eggplant slices.

- Cook the eggplant in the air fryer for 10 minutes, flipping once halfway through.

- Remove the eggplant from the air fryer and serve hot.

You can serve the gluten-free air fryer eggplant as a side dish or use it as a base for a variety of dishes, such as eggplant parmesan or eggplant roll-ups. Enjoy!

Chapter Eight: Desserts

These dishes will fulfill your sweet taste whether you follow a gluten-free diet or just want to try some delectable, healthier alternatives to classic fried treats.

You can experience all the crispy, crunchy goodness of fried foods without the extra fat and calories by using an air fryer. Additionally, it's a quick and simple method to whip up something delicious and filling in just a few minutes.

We have a wide range of delectable selections for you to taste, including fried fruit and churros as well as gluten-free cookies and donuts. Now let's start cooking with your air fryer!

Recipes:

Gluten-Free Air Fryer Apple Chips:

Whether you're trying to follow a gluten-free diet or just looking for a healthier alternative to traditional snacks, these apple chips are sure to become a favorite in your household.

Let's get started!

Ingredients

2 apples

1 teaspoon of cinnamon

1 tablespoon of sugar (optional)

Instructions:

- Preheat your air fryer to 350°F (180°C).

- Wash and thinly slice the apples into 1/4-inch rounds. You can use a mandoline slicer or a sharp knife to get even slices.

- In a small bowl, mix the cinnamon and sugar (if using).

- Coat the apple slices with the cinnamon mixture, making sure to evenly distribute the mixture on both sides of the slices.

- Place the coated apple slices in the air fryer basket in a single layer.

- Cook the apple slices for about 10-12 minutes or until they are crisp and golden brown.

- Remove the apple chips from the air fryer and let them cool before serving.

Enjoy your gluten-free air fryer apple chips as a healthy snack or dessert. You can also serve them with a dip or use them as a topping for oatmeal or yogurt.

Gluten-Free Air Fryer Chocolate Chip Cookies:

These cookies are made with a combination of almond and coconut flour, which give them a nutty flavor and a soft, chewy texture.
They're also made with dairy-free chocolate chips, making them suitable for those with dietary restrictions or allergies.

Ingredients:

1 cup almond flour
1/2 cup tapioca flour
1/2 tsp baking soda
1/4 tsp salt
1/2 cup unsalted butter, softened
1/2 cup granulated sugar
1/2 cup light brown sugar
1 large egg
1 tsp vanilla extract
1 cup chocolate chips

Instructions:

- In a medium bowl, whisk together the almond flour, tapioca flour, baking soda, and salt.

- In a separate large bowl, beat together the butter, granulated sugar, and brown sugar until smooth and creamy.

- Whip in the egg and vanilla extract.

- Slowly add the wet ingredients to the dry ingredients and mix until well incorporated.

- Stir in the chocolate chips.

- Preheat your air fryer to 350°F.

- Scoop the cookie dough into a 1 1/2-inch ball and place them on the air fryer basket, leaving about an inch of space between each cookie.

- You may need to work it batch by batch depending on the size of your air fryer.

- Cook the cookies in the air fryer for 7-9 minutes, until they are golden brown around the edges.

- Take out the cookies from the fryer and let them cool on a wire rack.

Enjoy!

Gluten-Free Air Fryer Brownies:

These fudgy, chocolatey treats are delicious and easy desserts that can be made in your air fryer.

With a simple list of ingredients, including gluten-free flour and cocoa powder, these brownies come together quickly and are ready to enjoy in no time.

Let's get started!

Ingredients

1 cup gluten-free flour
1 cup granulated sugar
1/2 cup unsweetened cocoa powder
1/2 cup vegetable oil
3 eggs
1 tsp vanilla extract
1/4 tsp salt

Once you have your ingredients, you can begin preparing the brownie mixture.

- In a big mixing bowl, whisk together the flour, sugar, cocoa powder, and salt until well incorporated.

- Add in the eggs, vegetable oil, and vanilla extract, and mix until everything is well combined and a smooth batter forms.

- Next, preheat your air fryer to 350°F.

- Pour the brownie mixture into a greased 8x8-inch baking pan, and place the pan in the air fryer.

- Cook the brownies for about 15-20 minutes, or until a toothpick inserted in the center comes out clean.

- Once the brownies are finished cooking, remove the pan from the air fryer and let it cool for a few minutes before slicing and serving.

These gluten-free air fryer brownies are moist and fudgy, with a rich chocolate flavor that will satisfy any sweet tooth. Enjoy!

Gluten-Free Air Fryer Banana Bread:

Here is a recipe for gluten-free banana bread that can be made in an air fryer:

Ingredients:

2 cups gluten-free flour blend
1 tsp baking powder
1 tsp baking soda
1/2 tsp salt
1/2 cup unsalted butter, melted
1 cup granulated sugar
3 large eggs, beaten
1 tsp vanilla extract
One cup mashed bananas (about 4 medium bananas)
1/2 cup milk

Instructions:

- In a medium bowl, whisk together the gluten-free flour blend, baking soda, salt, and baking powder.

- In a big bowl, whisk together the melted butter and sugar until nicely incorporated.

- Add the eggs and vanilla section to the butter and sugar combination, and whisk until well incorporated.

- Add the mashed bananas and milk to the mixture, and stir until well incorporated.

- Put in the wet ingredients with the dry ingredients and stir until just incorporated.

- Preheat your air fryer to 330°F (165°C).

- Turn the batter into a greased 9x5-inch loaf pan and smooth the top with a spatula.

- Set the pan in the air fryer and cook for 45-50 minutes, or until a toothpick inserted into the middle of the loaf comes out neat.

- Take out the pan from the air fryer and let the banana bread cool in the pan for 12 minutes.

- Transfer the banana bread to a wire rack to cool completely before slicing and serving.

I hope you enjoy this gluten-free banana bread made in the air fryer!

Gluten-Free Air Fryer Peach Crisp:

Here is a recipe for a gluten-free peach crisp made in an air fryer:

Ingredients:

3 cups peeled and sliced peaches
2 tablespoons cornstarch
2 tablespoons granulated sugar
1 teaspoon lemon juice
1/4 teaspoon cinnamon
1/4 cup rolled oats
1/4 cup almond flour
2 tablespoons brown sugar
2 tablespoons butter, melted
1/4 teaspoon salt

Instructions:

- In a medium bowl, mix the sliced peaches, cornstarch, granulated sugar, lemon juice, and cinnamon.

- In a separate small bowl, mix the rolled oats, almond flour, brown sugar, melted butter, and salt.

- Set the peach combination in the air fryer basket.

- Drizzle the oat combination over the top of the peaches.

- Set the air fryer to 350°F and cook for 15-20 minutes, or until the peaches are tender and the topping is golden brown.

- Serve warm with a spoon of ice cream or a bit of whipped cream, if you wish

This gluten-free peach crisp is a delicious and easy dessert that can be made in your air fryer.

The peaches are cooked to perfection and topped with a crispy and flavorful oat and almond flour topping.

It's a great way to enjoy a classic dessert without gluten. Enjoy!

Gluten-Free Air Fryer Peanut Butter Cookies:

Here is a recipe for peanut butter cookies made in an air fryer:

Ingredients:

1 cup creamy peanut butter

1 cup granulated sugar
1 large egg
1 teaspoon baking powder
1/2 teaspoon salt

Instructions:

- Preheat your air fryer to 355°F (180°C).

- In a medium together the peanut butter, sugar, egg, baking powder, and salt until well combined.

- Roll the dough into 1-inch balls and place them in the air fryer basket, leaving about 1 inch of space between each ball.

- Cook the cookies for 8-10 minutes, or until they are lightly golden brown.

- Take out the cookies from the fryer and let them cool on a wire rack.

Enjoy your delicious peanut butter cookies!

Note: If you don't have an air fryer, you can also bake these cookies in a preheated oven at 350°F (180°C) for 8-10 minutes.

Gluten-Free Air Fryer Donuts:

Ingredients:

One cup gluten-free flour blend
1/4 cup granulated sugar
1 tsp baking powder
1/2 tsp salt
1/2 cup milk (dairy or non-dairy)
1 egg
2 tbsp butter or oil, melted
1 tsp vanilla extract

Instructions:

- In a portable bowl, mix the flour, salt, baking powder, and sugar.

- In a different little bowl, whisk together the milk, egg melted butter or oil, and vanilla extract.

- Put the wet ingredients into the dry ingredients and stir until just blended.

- The batter should be thick but smooth.

- Spoon the batter into a plastic bag or a piping bag fitted with a large round tip.

- Preheat your air fryer to 350°F (180°C).

- Cut a small corner off of the plastic bag or pipe the batter into the air fryer basket, using a circular motion to form the donut shape.

- Cook the donuts in the air fryer for 5-6 minutes, or until they are puffed and lightly golden brown.

- Allow the donuts to cool for a few minutes before glazing or serving. Enjoy!

You can also try adding some flavor variations by stirring in some cocoa powder, spices, or fruit puree to the batter. You can also top the donuts with a simple glaze or sprinkle them with sugar or cocoa powder.

Gluten-Free Air Fryer Lemon Bars:

Gluten-free lemon bars are a delicious and refreshing treat that can be easily made in an air fryer.

To make gluten-free lemon bars, you will need the following ingredients:

Ingredients:

One cup of almond flour
2 tablespoons coconut flour
¼ teaspoon salt

2 tablespoons coconut oil, melted
2 tablespoons honey
1 egg
1 teaspoon vanilla extract
¾ cup coconut sugar
2 tablespoons cornstarch
1/3 cup lemon juice
2 eggs

Instructions:

- Preheat your air fryer to 350°F (180°C).

- In a portable bowl, mix the salt, coconut flour, and almond flour.

- Add in the coconut oil, honey, egg, and vanilla extract and mix until well combined.

- Press the mixture into the bottom of a greased 8x8-inch pan.

- In a separate bowl, mix the coconut sugar, cornstarch, lemon juice, and eggs until smooth.

- Pour the combination over the crust in the pan.

- Place the pan in the air fryer and cook for 15-20 minutes, or until the filling is set and the crust is golden brown.

- Allow the bars to cool before slicing and serving. Enjoy!

These gluten-free lemon bars are a tasty and easy dessert that everyone can enjoy.

They are perfect for a summertime treat or for any time you are craving something sweet and tangy.

Chapter Nine: Sauces Dressings and Staples

Air fryers are a popular appliance for cooking a variety of foods, including meats, vegetables, and even some desserts.
They work by circulating hot air around the food to create a crispy, crunchy texture, similar to deep frying, but without the need for as much oil.
This makes them a healthier option for cooking many types of foods.

When it comes to sauces, dressings, and staples that are suitable for a gluten-free diet, it's important to look for products that are specifically labeled as gluten-free.

Many common sauces and dressings contain wheat or other gluten-containing ingredients, so it's important to read labels carefully and choose those that are made with gluten-free ingredients.

Some examples of gluten-free sauces and dressings that can be prepared in an air fryer include marinades, BBQ sauces, and vinaigrettes.

In terms of staples, many gluten-free options can be prepared in an air fryer, including grains like quinoa, rice, and oats, as well as vegetables and proteins like chicken, beef, and seafood.

These can be combined with a variety of sauces and dressings to create a wide range of delicious, gluten-free meals that can be cooked quickly and easily in an air fryer.

So, with a little bit of planning and the right ingredients, it's possible to create a variety of tasty, gluten-free meals using an air fryer.

Recipes:

Gluten-Free Air Fryer Barbeque Sauce:

Gluten-free barbeque sauce can be easily made in an air fryer using gluten-free ingredients.

Below is a recipe you can try:

Ingredients:

1 cup tomato sauce
1/2 cup apple cider vinegar
1/4 cup brown sugar
1/4 cup molasses
2 tablespoons gluten-free Worcestershire sauce
1 tablespoon paprika
1 teaspoon garlic powder
1 teaspoon onion powder
1/2 teaspoon salt

Instructions:

- In a small saucepan, combine all ingredients and stir to combine.

- Heat the sauce over medium heat, stirring occasionally, until it comes to a boil.

- Reduce the heat to low and simmer for 10-15 minutes, or until the sauce has thickened to your desired consistency.

- Transfer the sauce to the bowl of your air fryer and set the temperature to 350°F.

- Cook the sauce for 5-10 minutes, or until it has reached your desired thickness.

- Use the sauce immediately or transfer it to a jar and store it in the refrigerator for later use.

This gluten-free barbeque sauce can be used to marinate and flavor meats and vegetables before cooking them in the air fryer. It can also be used as a topping for sandwiches, burgers, or other dishes. Enjoy!

Gluten-Free Ranch Air Fryer Dressing:

Gluten-free ranch dressing is a tasty and creamy condiment that can be made easily in an air fryer.
Here is a simple recipe for gluten-free ranch dressing that can be made in an air fryer:

Ingredients:

1 cup mayonnaise (make sure it is gluten-free)
1/2 cup sour cream (make sure it is gluten-free)
1/2 cup milk (any kind will do)
1/4 cup diced fresh chives
2 tablespoons diced fresh dill
2 cloves garlic, minced
1 teaspoon onion powder
1/2 teaspoon salt
1/4 teaspoon black pepper

Instructions:

- In a small mixing bowl, whisk together the mayonnaise, sour cream, and milk until smooth.

- Add the chives, dill, garlic, onion powder, salt, and pepper to the bowl and mix well.

- Pour the dressing into a small air fryer-safe container or jar.

- Place the container or jar in the air fryer and cook at 350°F for 5-7 minutes, or until the dressing is heated through and slightly bubbly.

- Remove the container or jar from the air fryer and let it cool for a few minutes before serving.

This gluten-free ranch dressing is perfect for dipping vegetables, spreading on sandwiches, or tossing with salads.

It can be stored in the refrigerator for up to a week, so you can make a batch and enjoy it throughout the week. Enjoy!

Gluten-Free Air Fryer Lemon Vinaigrette:

Ingredients:

2 tablespoons lemon juice
1 tablespoon olive oil
1 teaspoon Dijon mustard
1 small clove of garlic and, minced
Salt and pepper, to taste

Instructions:

- In a small bowl, whisk together the lemon juice, olive oil, Dijon mustard, and minced garlic.

- Season with salt and pepper to taste.

- Place your desired vegetables in the air fryer basket and spray them with cooking spray.

- Cook the vegetables in the air fryer at 400°F for about 10-15 minutes, or until they are tender and caramelized.

- Remove the vegetables from the air fryer and drizzle with the lemon vinaigrette.

Serve and enjoy!

This vinaigrette is a great way to add flavor to your air fryer vegetables, and it is also gluten-free, making it suitable for those with gluten sensitivities or celiac disease.

The lemon juice and Dijon mustard give the vinaigrette a tangy and slightly spicy flavor, while the olive oil helps to smooth out the flavors and add richness.

The minced garlic adds a subtle hint of warmth and depth of flavor. The vinaigrette is also quick and easy to prepare, making it a convenient option for a healthy and flavorful meal.

Gluten-Free Air Fryer Teriyaki Sauce:

Gluten-free teriyaki sauce is a flavorful and savory sauce that is commonly used in Asian cuisine. It is made with a combination of soy sauce, sugar, garlic, and ginger, and is often used as a marinade or a finishing sauce for grilled or fried meats and vegetables.

ingredients:

1/2 cup gluten-free soy sauce or tamari
1/2 cup sugar

1 clove garlic, minced
1 teaspoon grated ginger
2 tablespoons water

Instructions

- combine the soy sauce, sugar, garlic, and ginger in a small saucepan over medium heat.

- Convey the combination to a boil, then reduce the heat to low and simmer for 4 or 5 minutes.

- Add the water and continue to simmer for an additional 2-3 minutes, until the sauce has thickened slightly.

- Once the sauce is ready, you can use it as a marinade for your air fryer chicken, pork, or vegetables.

- Simply coat your protein or vegetables in the sauce and let it marinate for at least 30 minutes before cooking.

You can also brush the sauce on your protein or vegetables while they are cooking in the air fryer, or use it as a finishing sauce once they are cooked.
Enjoy your gluten-free teriyaki sauce in your air fryer dishes!

Gluten-free air fryer pesto:

Gluten-free air fryer pesto is a delicious and easy-to-make recipe that can be made using an air fryer.

Pesto is a traditional Italian sauce made from basil, pine nuts, garlic, and Parmesan cheese, and is often used as a condiment or a spread for sandwiches and pasta.

Ingredients

2 cups fresh basil leaves
1/2 cup pine nuts
1/2 cup grated Parmesan cheese
2 cloves garlic
1/2 cup olive oil
Salt and pepper to taste

Instructions

- simply combine the basil, pine nuts, Parmesan cheese, and garlic in a blender or food processor and pulse until the ingredients are finely chopped.

- Slowly add the olive oil and blend until the mixture becomes smooth and creamy. Flavor with pepper and salt.

- To air fry the pesto, place a small amount of the sauce in an air fryer basket and set the temperature to 375°F (190°C).

- Cook for about 3-5 minutes, or until the pesto is heated through and slightly crispy on the edges.

Serve the gluten-free air fryer pesto as a condiment for sandwiches, and pasta, or as a spread for crackers or bread.
It can also be used as a marinade for grilled chicken or vegetables. Enjoy!

Gluten-free air fryer buffalo sauce:

Ingredients

1/2 cup of Frank's RedHot sauce (or your preferred hot sauce)
2 tablespoons of unsalted butter
2 cloves of garlic, minced
1/4 teaspoon of paprika
1/4 teaspoon of onion powder
1/4 teaspoon of cayenne pepper
Salt and pepper to taste

Instructions

- dissolve the butter in a tiny saucepan over medium heat.

- Put in the minced garlic and cook for 3 minutes.

- Add the hot sauce, paprika, onion powder, cayenne pepper, salt, and pepper, and stir to combine.

- Bring the mixture to a simmer and cook for an additional 2-3 minutes, until the sauce has thickened slightly.

- To use the sauce in an air fryer, preheat the air fryer to 400°F.

- Place your desired protein (such as chicken wings or tenders) in the air fryer basket and spray it with cooking spray.

- Cook the protein for 8-10 minutes, until it is cooked through and crispy.

- Once the protein is cooked, remove it from the air fryer and toss it in the gluten-free buffalo sauce until it is evenly coated.

- Return the coated protein to the air fryer basket and cook for an additional 2-3 minutes, until the sauce is hot and bubbly.

Serve the protein with the buffalo sauce and your desired side dishes and enjoy!

Chapter Ten: Meat and Seafood

Gluten-free air fryer meat and seafood dishes can be a delicious and convenient option for those following a gluten-free diet or looking to incorporate more gluten-free meals into their routine.

Many gluten-free options for meat and seafood can be cooked in an air fryer, such as chicken, beef, pork, fish, and shellfish.

These dishes can be marinated, coated in a gluten-free breading or seasoning, or simply cooked on their own.

Gluten-free sauces and dips can also be used to add flavor to the finished dish.

Cooking with a gluten-free air fryer can be a simple and delicious way to enjoy a variety of meat and seafood dishes while following a gluten-free diet.

Whether you are looking for a quick and easy weeknight dinner or a tasty party appetizer, there are endless options for gluten-free air fryer meat and seafood dishes to suit your needs.

Recipes:

Gluten-Free Air Fryer Chicken Tenders:

Gluten-free air fryer chicken tenders are a delicious and healthy alternative to traditional fried chicken tenders.

They are made with gluten-free flour and breadcrumbs and are cooked in an air fryer instead of being deep-fried.

This results in a crispy and flavorful chicken tender that is much lower in fat and calories than its deep-fried counterpart.

Ingredients

1 pound of boneless, skinless chicken breasts
1 cup of gluten-free flour
1 cup of gluten-free breadcrumbs
1 teaspoon of salt
1 teaspoon of pepper
1 teaspoon of garlic powder
2 eggs
2 tablespoons of milk

Instructions

- trim the chicken breasts into thin strips and put them aside.

- In a shallow dish, mix the gluten-free flour, breadcrumbs, salt, pepper, and garlic powder.

- In a separate shallow dish, beat the eggs and milk together.

- Dip each chicken strip into the egg mixture, then coat it with the gluten-free flour mixture.

- Place the coated chicken strips in the air fryer basket, making sure they are not touching.

- Cook the chicken tenders in the air fryer at 400°F for 8-10 minutes, or until they are cooked through and crispy.

- Serve the chicken tenders with your choice of dipping sauce and enjoy!

Some variations on this recipe include using almond flour or coconut flour in place of the gluten-free flour or adding some seasoning of your choice to the flour mixture (such as Italian seasoning or paprika). You can also try using chicken thighs or tenders in place of the breasts for a different flavor and texture.

Gluten-Free Air Fryer Shrimp:

here is a recipe for gluten-free air fryer shrimp:

Ingredients:

1 pound large shrimp, peeled and deveined
2 tablespoons olive oil
1 teaspoon garlic powder

1 teaspoon paprika
1/2 teaspoon salt
1/4 teaspoon black pepper

Instructions:

- Preheat your air fryer to 400°F.

- In a small bowl, mix the olive oil, garlic powder, paprika, salt, and pepper.

- Place the shrimp in a large bowl and toss with the spice mixture until well coated.

- Place the shrimp in the air fryer basket in a single layer, making sure not to overcrowd the basket.

- Cook the shrimp for 8-10 minutes, or until they are pink and fully cooked.

Serve the shrimp hot, with your choice of dipping sauce, or as part of a larger meal.

Tips:
If you don't have an air fryer, you can also cook the shrimp in the oven. Preheat the oven to 400°F and bake the coated shrimp on a baking sheet for 8-10 minutes, or until they are pink and fully cooked.

To make this recipe gluten-free, be sure to use gluten-free spices and check the label on the shrimp to make sure they were not processed in a facility that also handles gluten-containing ingredients.

Gluten-Free Air Fryer Pork Chops:

here is a recipe for gluten-free pork chops that can be cooked in an air fryer:

Ingredients:

4 pork chops, about 1 inch thick
1 teaspoon paprika
1 teaspoon garlic powder
1 teaspoon onion powder
1/2 teaspoon salt
1/4 teaspoon black pepper
1/4 cup olive oil

Instructions:

- Preheat your air fryer to 400°F.

- Prepare a small bowl and mix the paprika, salt, garlic powder, pepper, and onion powder.

- Brush each pork chop with olive oil, then sprinkle the spice mixture over both sides of the pork chops.

- Position the pork chops in the fryer basket, making sure they are not touching.

- Cook the pork chops for 10-12 minutes, flipping them halfway through until they reach an internal temperature of 145 degrees Fahrenheit.

Remove the pork chops from the air fryer and let them rest for a few minutes before serving.

Enjoy your gluten-free pork chops!

Gluten-Free Air Fryer Salmon:

Air fryers are a convenient and efficient way to cook a variety of dishes, including gluten-free salmon. Here is a simple recipe for preparing gluten-free salmon in an air fryer:

Ingredients:

4 (6-ounce) salmon filets
2 tablespoons olive oil
1/2 teaspoon salt
1/4 teaspoon black pepper
2 cloves garlic, minced
2 tablespoons lemon juice
1 teaspoon Dijon mustard

Instructions:

- Preheat your air fryer to 400°F.

- In a small bowl, whisk together the olive oil, salt, pepper, garlic, lemon juice, and mustard to create a marinade.

- Place the salmon filets in a shallow dish and brush them with the marinade. Marinate the salmon for about 12 minutes.

- Place the salmon filets in the air fryer basket, making sure to leave enough space between each filet.

- Cook the salmon for about 9 minutes, or until it is cooked to the level of doneness you desire.

- Serve the salmon with your choices of gluten-free sides, such as roasted vegetables or a salad.

Note: If you are following a strict gluten-free diet, be sure to double-check that all of the ingredients you use are certified gluten-free.

Some seasonings and condiments may contain gluten, so it is important to read labels carefully.

Gluten-Free Air Fryer Turkey:

A gluten-free air fryer turkey breast is a delicious and convenient way to enjoy turkey without worrying about gluten.

Ingredients:

1 turkey breast, about 2-3 pounds
1 tablespoon olive oil
1 teaspoon sea salt
1/2 teaspoon black pepper
1/2 teaspoon paprika
1/2 teaspoon garlic powder
1/2 teaspoon onion powder

Instructions:

- Preheat your air fryer to 400°F.

- In a portable bowl, combine the pepper, paprika, garlic powder, onion powder, and salt.

- Rub the turkey breast all over with the olive oil, then sprinkle the seasoning mixture over the top.

- Set the turkey breast in the air fryer basket and cook for 20 minutes.

- Rotate the turkey breast over and cook for an extra 10-15 minutes, or until the internal temperature reaches 165°F.

- Remove the turkey breast from the air fryer and let it rest for 5-10 minutes before slicing and serving.

Serve the turkey breast with your favorite gluten-free side dishes, such as roasted vegetables or a salad. Enjoy!

Gluten-Free Air Fryer Crab Cakes:

Gluten-free crab cakes are a tasty and healthy alternative to traditional crab cakes, which are often made with wheat flour.

They can be made in an air fryer, which is a kitchen appliance that uses hot air to cook food.

Air fryers are a great way to cook crab cakes because they provide a crispy exterior without the need for deep frying.

Ingredients:

1 pound fresh crab meat
1 egg
1/2 cup gluten-free bread crumbs
1/4 cup mayonnaise
2 tablespoons Dijon mustard
1 teaspoon Old Bay seasoning
1/4 teaspoon salt
1/4 teaspoon black pepper
2 tablespoons olive oil or cooking spray (for the air fryer)

Instructions:

- In a medium bowl, mix the crab meat, egg, gluten-free bread crumbs, mayonnaise, Dijon mustard, Old Bay seasoning, salt, and pepper.

- Use the mixture to form small patties, about 1/2 inch thick.

- Place the patties in the air fryer basket and brush with olive oil or spray with cooking spray.

- Set the air fryer to 400°F and cook the crab cakes for 8-10 minutes, until they are golden brown and crispy.

- Serve the crab cakes with a side of tartar dressing or your favorite dipping sauce.

You can also add other ingredients to the crab cake mixture, such as minced onions, diced bell peppers, or chopped herbs, to add flavor and texture.

These gluten-free crab cakes make a delicious appetizer or main dish, and they are a healthier alternative to traditional crab cakes. Enjoy!

Gluten-Free Air Fryer Cod Filets:

Gluten-free air fryer cod filets can be a delicious and healthy option for people who are following a gluten-free diet or who are sensitive to gluten.

Cod is a type of white fish that is low in fat and high in protein, making it a healthy choice for a variety of meals.

To make gluten-free cod filets in an air fryer, you will need:

1. Cod filets (4-6 ounces each)

2. Gluten-free flour or cornstarch

3. Salt and pepper

4. Olive oil or cooking spray

To begin,

- Preheat your air fryer to 400°F.

- While the air fryer is heating up, season the cod filets with salt and pepper.

- coat the filets in gluten-free flour or cornstarch, making sure to evenly coat both sides. This will help create a crispy crust on the outside of the fish.

- Spray the basket of the air fryer with cooking spray or brush with a light coating of olive oil.

- Place the cod filets in the basket, making sure they are not crowded or overlapping.

- Cook the filets for 8-10 minutes, or until the fish is cooked through and flakes easily with a fork.

Serve the gluten-free air fryer cod filets with your choice of sides and toppings.

Some options could include a salad, roasted vegetables, or a simple garlic and lemon sauce. Enjoy!

Chapter Eleven: Tips and Tricks for Gluten-Free Air Fryer Cooking

If you're someone who follows a gluten-free diet, you may have found that traditional frying methods can be difficult to navigate.

That's where the air fryer comes in! This handy kitchen appliance uses hot air to cook and crisp up a variety of foods, including those that are gluten-free.
In this guide, you will get some tips and tricks to help you get the most out of your air fryer when cooking gluten-free meals.

From choosing the right ingredients to finding the perfect cooking time and temperature, we've got you covered.

So let's get started!

If you are following a gluten-free diet and want to use an air fryer to prepare your meals, these are a few tips and tricks you can follow to ensure success.

Choose gluten-free ingredients:
The most important thing to remember when cooking gluten-free in an air fryer is to choose naturally gluten-free ingredients. This includes fresh vegetables, meats, poultry, and seafood, as well as gluten-free grains like rice, quinoa, and corn.

Use a gluten-free coating:

If you are breading or coating your food, make sure to use a gluten-free breadcrumb or flour mix. There are many gluten-free options available at most grocery stores or you can make your own by grinding up gluten-free oats or rice in a food processor.

Check for hidden sources of gluten:
Some ingredients, like soy sauce and Worcestershire sauce, can contain gluten, so be sure to read labels carefully and choose gluten-free options.

Use a separate basket:
If you are cooking multiple items at once and some contain gluten, it is a good idea to use a separate basket for the gluten-free items to avoid cross-contamination.

Preheat the air fryer:
Preheating the air fryer can help ensure that your food cooks evenly and achieves the desired level of crispiness.

By following these tips, you can enjoy delicious and satisfying gluten-free meals prepared in your air fryer.

Here are a few tips for successful gluten-free air fryer cooking:

Use gluten-free flours and breadcrumbs:
Instead of wheat flour, try using gluten-free alternatives like almond flour, coconut flour, or rice flour. Look for gluten-free breadcrumbs or make your own by pulsing gluten-free bread in a food processor.

Check labels:

Always double-check the labels of any pre-packaged ingredients to ensure they are gluten-free.

Be aware of cross-contamination:
If you are using the same air fryer for both gluten-free and non-gluten-free foods, make sure to thoroughly clean the appliance between uses to avoid cross-contamination.

With a little bit of planning and these tips in mind, you can enjoy all the deliciousness of air fryer cooking without having to worry about gluten. Happy cooking!

Gluten-Free Flour and Breading Options:

Gluten-free flour is a type of flour that does not contain gluten, a protein found in wheat, barley, and rye.

Gluten-free flour is often made from alternative grains, such as rice, corn, quinoa, or beans, and is used to make bread, pasta, and other baked goods for people who are sensitive to or allergic to gluten.

There are many different types of gluten-free flour available on the market, and each type has its unique properties and characteristics.

For example, rice flour is light and powdery, while bean flours are heavier and have a stronger flavor.

Some gluten-free flours are also fortified with additional nutrients, such as vitamins and minerals, to make them nutritionally similar to wheat flour.

In addition to using gluten-free flour to make bread and other baked goods, it can also be used as a breading for fried foods.

To use gluten-free flour as a breading, simply mix it with a little water or milk to create a smooth, sticky batter, and then coat the food in the batter before frying.

Other options for gluten-free breading include cornmeal, potato flakes, and ground nuts or seeds.

It is important to note that gluten-free breading options may not have the same texture or crunch as breading made with wheat flour, but they can still be used to add flavor and a crispy coating to fried foods.

It may also be necessary to adjust the cooking time or temperature when using gluten-free breading, as the ingredients may cook differently than wheat flour.

Gluten-Free Sauce and Seasoning Ideas:

There are many gluten-free sauce and seasoning options available for those who need to avoid gluten in their diet. Here are a few ideas:

Tomato sauce:

Many store-bought tomato sauces are naturally gluten-free, but it's always a good idea to double-check the label to make sure. You can also make your tomato sauce at home using gluten-free ingredients.

BBQ sauce:

There are many gluten-free BBQ sauces available at the grocery store, or you can make your own using gluten-free ingredients such as tomato sauce, apple cider vinegar, honey, and a variety of spices.

Soy sauce:

Traditional soy sauce contains gluten, but there are many gluten-free alternatives available. Look for tamari, which is made from fermented soybeans, or coconut aminos, which are made from coconut sap and sea salt.

Hot Sauce:

Many hot sauces are naturally gluten-free, but it's always a good idea to check the label to be sure. Sriracha and chili garlic sauce are both gluten-free options.

Pesto:

Pesto is a sauce made from basil, pine nuts, garlic, and olive oil. It is usually gluten-free, but it's always a good idea to check the label or make your own using gluten-free ingredients.

Ranch dressing:

Many store-bought ranch dressings contain gluten, but it is easy to make your gluten-free version using mayonnaise, sour cream, and a variety of spices.

Spices:

Most spices are naturally gluten-free, so feel free to use them as much as you like to add flavor to your meals. Some prevalent options are onion, garlic, paprika, chili powder, and cumin.

Remember to always check labels and ingredient lists when shopping for gluten-free sauces and seasonings.

How to adjust traditional recipes to be made in an air fryer

Here's how to modify conventional recipes so they can be prepared in an air fryer:

Adjust the cooking time and temperature: When converting a recipe to air fryer cooking, you'll need to adjust the cooking time and temperature. Air fryers cook food quickly, so you'll need to reduce the cooking time and lower the temperature by about 25 degrees Fahrenheit compared to conventional cooking methods. Start with the recommended air fryer cooking time and temperature, and adjust as needed to get the desired results.

Use a light coating of oil or cooking spray: While air fryers use less oil than conventional frying methods, you'll still need to use some oil to achieve a crispy exterior. Instead of soaking your food in oil, use a light coating of oil or cooking spray. You can also try using non-stick cooking spray or silicone baking mats to prevent sticking.

Cut your ingredients into smaller pieces: To ensure that your food cooks evenly and thoroughly in the air fryer, cut your ingredients into smaller pieces. This will also help to reduce the cooking time and ensure that your food cooks through.

Preheat the air fryer: Just like a conventional oven, preheating your air fryer will help to ensure even cooking and a crispy exterior. Preheat the air fryer for a few minutes before adding your food, and adjust the cooking time accordingly.

Experiment with different ingredients and seasonings: One of the great things about air fryer cooking is that you can experiment with different ingredients and seasonings to create a wide range of flavors and textures. Try adding different herbs and spices to your favorite recipes, or experiment with different types of oil for a unique flavor profile.

By making these simple modifications, you can easily convert your favorite conventional recipes to air fryer cooking. Not only will you be able to enjoy all your favorite dishes with a healthier twist, but you'll also be able to do it quickly and easily with an air fryer. So go ahead and give it a try – your taste buds (and your waistline) will thank you!

Troubleshooting Common Gluten-Free Air Fryer Problems:

Here are some common problems that may occur when using a gluten-free air fryer and some possible solutions:

Food not cooking evenly:
Make sure that the food is placed in a single layer in the basket and that it is not overcrowded. Also, shake the basket halfway through cooking to redistribute the food.

Food sticking to the basket:
Make sure to spray the basket with cooking spray or lightly coat it with oil before adding the food. You can also try using a liner or parchment paper to prevent sticking.

Food not getting crispy:
Make sure the air fryer is preheated before adding the food and that the temperature and cooking time is set correctly. You can also try using a higher temperature or cooking for a longer period.

Food burning:
Keep an eye on the food while it is cooking and use a meat thermometer to check for doneness. You may need to adjust the cooking period and temperature.

Air fryer not turning on:

Make sure the air fryer is plugged in and that the outlet is functioning properly. If the air fryer still doesn't turn on, check the fuse or circuit breaker.

Air fryer not heating up:
Make sure the air fryer is set to the correct temperature and that the heating element is not damaged. If the air fryer still doesn't heat up, it may need to be repaired or replaced.

If these troubleshooting tips don't resolve the issue, it may be helpful to refer to the manufacturer's instructions or contact customer service for further assistance.

The Versatility of Gluten-Free Air Fryer Cooking:

These dishes will fulfill your sweet taste whether you follow a gluten-free diet or just want to try some delectable, healthier alternatives to classic fried treats.

You can experience all the crispy, crunchy goodness of fried foods without the extra fat and calories by using an air fryer. Additionally, it's a quick and simple method to whip up something delicious and filling in just a few minutes.

We have a wide range of delectable selections for you to taste, including fried fruit and churros as well as gluten-free cookies and donuts. Now let's start cooking with your air fryer!

The air fryer's ability to prepare a wide range of gluten-free foods is one of its many wonderful features. For instance, you can roast veggies or prepare crispy, gluten-free fried chicken with it. Additionally, you may use it to create gluten-free variations of traditional foods like fish and chips and onion rings.

The air fryer is not only adaptable, but also practical and simple to operate. It is ideal for busy people or families because it heats up quickly and requires minimum cleanup.

In general, the air fryer is a useful appliance for anyone wishing to increase the amount of gluten-free foods in their diet. Anyone wishing to learn more about gluten-free cooking will find it to be an excellent choice due to its diversity, practicality, and simplicity of use.

Made in the USA
Coppell, TX
25 April 2023